Rick Jolly qualified as a doctor from Saint Bartholomew's Hospital, London, in 1969 and joined the Royal Navy in 1971. He spent the majority of the next 25 years as a Commando medical officer with the Royal Marines, and as a Flight Surgeon with the Fleet Air Arm. Operationally, he has had wide experience. Three winters in Norway stimulated an interest in cold weather injuries, a speciality which proved useful in 1982 when he commanded the field hospital set up at Ajax Bay during the Falklands War. The great success of this unit – only three of nearly 600 injured in the land battles subsequently died of their wounds – was recognised by the award of an OBE in the South Atlantic Honours List.

His book *The Red and Green Life Machine* told the story of the Ajax Bay facility, while *JACKSPEAK* is a humorous anthology of Royal Navy and Royal Marines slang. His other professional publications are concerned with patterns of wounding during the land battles of the Falklands Conflict, and analysis of the fantastically low mortality figures.

As Chairman of the South Atlantic Medal Association (1982) he has been deeply involved with the start-up and initial running of this vitally important group. He will be donating all his royalties from *IN CONFIDENCE* to SAMA82, and intends to do the same with an on-going revision of *JACKSPEAK*.

IN CONFIDENCE
ISBN 0 9514305 1 3

Published in Great Britain by FoSAMA Books,
an imprint of Palamanando Press.

Printing history
FoSAMA paperback edition published 1997

Set in 14 on 16 point Garamond Light.
Origination by the author using an Acorn RISC PC,
transferred to *QuarkXpress*, then prepared for print by
Curtis Alcock on an Apple Power Macintosh. Imageset
and produced by Design and Print Limited,
Plympton, PL7 5HQ, Devon.

**FoSAMA Books are published by Palamanando
Press, PO Box 42, Torpoint, Cornwall PL11 2YR**

IN CONFIDENCE

THE
JACKSPEAK
TRISERVICE GUIDE
TO STAFF REPORTING

by

RICK JOLLY

Dedicated to the 252 South Atlantic Task Force personnel who sailed from England in 1982 but did not return, and to the three Falkland Islanders who also died during the fight for their liberation.

From the sea – **Freedom**

CONTENTS

INTRODUCTION

In organisations containing large numbers of personnel, there has always been a need for an employee reporting system. Achievement, talent and potential need to be recognised, assessed and recorded. This observation has been especially true for the Armed Forces of the Crown. Until recently, it was even possible for a young man to join the Royal Navy as an ordinary seaman and then rise to Admiral's rank, thanks to the recognition and nurture of talent.

Although reporting systems are subject to a constant process of review, change and (hopefully) improvement, there is still scope for a sense of humour. Whenever discussion in a Royal Navy Wardroom, or an Army or Royal Air Force Officers Mess turns to the subject of confidential reporting, someone will usually remember some funny 'one-liners' that they have heard. While a few of these were included in *JACKSPEAK – A Guide to RN Slanguage,* it was felt that a more expanded collection might be a useful fund raiser for the South Atlantic Medal Association (SAMA).

This group, of which I am Chairman, was formed on April 2nd 1997. It aims to represent the interests of just under 30,000 veterans of Operation CORPORATE, and to generate closer links with the

Falkland Islanders for whom they risked their lives in 1982.

We were deeply honoured last Saturday when six of us, including three severely wounded veterans, were given a place of honour at the funeral of Diana, Princess of Wales, in Westminster Abbey. We very much agreed with her feelings about the indiscriminate use of landmines. During the service, I also thought back to those amazing days in Stanley, when Her Majesty's Sovereignty was restored to the Islands in the same June week that the wife of the Sovereign's Heir was delivered of a first-born son, and remembered the magic that she had worked amongst the injured of 1982, in the three Service Hospitals, and at Receptions for the men of her husband's Regiments. She shortened their convalescence and speeded their recovery with kind words and a dazzling smile.

May she rest in peace.

It was also felt that the scope of such a book might be widened, not just to include a rich haul of observations built up by the Royal Navy's Officer and Divisional reporting system, but to gather in those of the other two Armed Services as well. I am therefore extremely grateful to the Royal Air Force Air Secretary's Department (especially Squadron Leader John Harrison) for allowing me access to the light blue version of their 'Horrors and Howlers' collection. The recently retired Army Military Secretary, Major General Mike Scott CB DSO (himself a most distinguished South Atlantic veteran), sent in some very funny remarks from his own 'Black Book'. Some of these said much more about the Reporting Officer than the subject!

In addition to the sources already mentioned, I am grateful to friends and colleagues who have made both comments about, and contributions to this little book. From the Royal Navy, Captain Angus Sinclair has been particularly helpful. He is living proof of the old adage that if you want something done, ask a busy man. Commanders Philip Shaw MVO, George Zambellas and Philip Mathias MBE have also been kind critics and sources, as has Dennis Silverwood of Tavistock. Warrant Officer Keith Harrison and his team in the Drafting and Records Section of HQ Royal Marines have also been enthusiastic helpers.

I would also like to point out that I have tried to avoid grossly sexist remarks regarding appearance, beauty or age. There is something delicious about the statement *'If they put the right number of candles on her birthday cake, it would constitute a fire hazard'*, but this is an unlikely comment to have been made in a Service context. The TriService nature of the first edition is obvious. Perhaps in a future version, there may be some dilution into the non-military world under other headings. By then, such changes might require the title *IN CONFIDENCE* to be transformed as *The Jackspeak Book of Insults*.

So, all the comments reproduced here have

been made sometime and somewhere, in speech or on paper, and in a military context. You will note that some refer to those who are more senior in the chain of command, or to their spouses. These remarks have been left in, even though none of the Services yet has a system in which juniors report on their seniors. In every case, however, identity has been 'sanitized' with the use of different initials, and an attempt also made (where possible) to distribute both the ranks and parent service as evenly as possible.

If anyone reading this book recognises himself or herself in any of the descriptions, I can only say that guilt is in the eye of the beholder! As far as the author and publisher are concerned, all the people described in this book are fictitious, and any resemblance to actual persons living or dead is purely coincidental. Readers might be surprised at the need to make such a standard declaration, but they would have been equally taken aback, as I was recently, when contacted by the Reader's Digest HQ from Chicago. In condensing a magazine article which identified some *JACKSPEAK*-sourced Confidential Reports, their lady representative wanted to know exactly who the reports had been made about, in order to seek their permission to publish! The word 'apocryphal' did not appear to be part of her normal vocabulary.

I agree that some of the descriptions have a cutting edge which would now be described as far from 'Politically Correct'. Personally, I prefer the affectionate humour of someone being described as having *'duck's disease'* (short legs and a backside positioned close to the floor) than the more modern 'weasel word' phraseology of *'vertically challenged'*. Language is designed to convey meaning, and we should not shy from precision and accuracy, even if the truth hurts. If a report writer spent his time trying to avoid giving offence, then he might end up with a system approaching the American military model. Here, it seems that many of the personnel not actually grossly incompetent are described as 'outstanding'. This may make everyone involved feel good, but how on earth is such a system going to recognise the true high flyers and leaders of the future if mediocrity is considered good enough?

No doubt, some software whizzkid is currently hard at work constructing an Employee Assessment package which will do all the hard work for you. As the Reporting Officer, you'll just key in the final desired numerical percentage assessment, select a few appropriate descriptive qualities from a menu, and then sit back while the PC (Personal Computer) constructs a PC (Politically Correct) virtual assessment in its silicon memory. God forbid!

Needless to say, one Royal Navy chum has already suggested that this book should also be available on floppy disk – in order to make his reporting duties easier...

I hope you enjoy this little collection which has been built up over 25 years of careful listening, reading and recording during my time as a doctor in the Royal Navy. If you are ever required to write a staff report, whatever line of business you are in, you may also be able to adapt some of these comments to your own needs, especially on or around April 1st each year.

If you do, please acknowledge your source when or wherever you can. Better still, encourage others to buy this book and help us to maintain the South Atlantic Medal Association's aims and interests. You can order direct from the publishers, who will send my author's royalty, plus £1 per book sold, directly to SAMA82's Treasurer. For each copy retailing via the book trade, a smaller sum will accrue.

Also included, in an Appendix, is some useful information about the new South Atlantic Medal Association, plus information on how to contact the Secretary. We will be happy to send our colour leaflet and an application form if you qualify for one of its various Membership categories, which includes Affiliate Membership for our supporters who did not participate in 1982, but who love the Islands, the Islanders and their way of life.

If you can think of any additional entries suitable for inclusion under the personal characteristics that have been selected, then please send them in. There is some extra space at the back of the book for you to record your flashes of inspiration as they occur. All contributions will be acknowledged, and – if accepted – also rewarded in kind. Many thanks, in anticipation...

Finally, here's a wonderfully crafted cartoon drawn by my friend Tugg, and taken from *JACKSPEAK*. It is a requirement for all adverse comments about ratings in the Royal Navy to be read to them whenever periodic reports are rendered, and that these failings or deficiencies must then be underlined in red ink. Sometimes, the resulting irony can be delicious...

Rick Jolly
8th September 1997

ADAPTABILITY

One is tempted to suggest that he ought to get married. However, Pilot Officer Q is already married, and his charming young wife must think that she has three children rather than two.

My Adjutant is always down on everything that he is not up on.

A dithering and indecisive person, Lieutenant Q tends to wear the impression of the last person who sat on him.

Midshipman F started at the bottom and has stayed there.

The Commander-in-Chief tends to conclude discussion with a statement that his mind is already made up, and he does not want to be confused with the facts.

An aptitude test showed that this recruit's only real aptitude is for taking aptitude tests.

This Exchange Officer is a carefree sort of person who does not care much – just as long as it's free.

The Admiral is a typical senior executive who throughout his career has delegated all authority, shifted all the blame, but taken all the credit.

As an after dinner speaker, Colonel K can usually rise to the occasion, but then never knows when to sit down.

Squadron Leader G is like stodgy suet pudding – very difficult to digest.

This young man is about as useful as half a pair of scissors.

Midshipman D breezes through life in an untroubled manner. I am not sure whether it is indifference or inexperience that puts him beyond the reach of anxiety.

With more maturity, training and hard work, this Royal Marine recruit could make it as a civilian in due course, though not an outstanding one. At present, we feel that he could only be employed usefully as a torpedo tube pull-through.

ALCOHOL

This Leading Stoker is suffering from bottle fatigue.

Life for the Canteen Manager is a succession of burps and downs.

Lieutenant Commander P drinks like a fish, but unfortunately he does not drink what fishes drink.

When our Royal Marine adviser drinks, he tends to lose his inhibitions – and then give exhibitions.

His favourite drink is the next one.

The Senior Dental Officer's wife is forceful and garrulous, but well meaning. There have been occasions however when I have wished someone would give her a bottle of gin and a humane killer to play with.

My Surgeon Lieutenant is spoiling his own health by drinking to everyone else's.

The Buffer* usually drinks doubles – and then sees the same way.

Squadron Leader F is struggling manfully with a drink problem; the good news is that his wife is sticking to him through thick and gin.

I have occasionally seen this Officer sober.

Our Wine Caterer doesn't only drink, he also drinks between drinks.

When pink elephants get drunk, they see him.

This young Marine never drinks more than he can stand, and as soon as he can stand, he then starts drinking again.

Commander Q might be able to make both ends meet – if he wasn't so busy making one end drink.

If a mosquito bit my MEO**, it would probably die of alcohol poisoning.

The Supply Officer magnifies his troubles by looking at them through the bottom of a glass.

This Marine behaved so outrageously on a run ashore last week that even his shock-proof watch was embarrassed.

---

* Buffer – the Senior Seamanship Specialist rating in a warship.
** Marine Engineer Officer.

As President of the Wardroom Wine Tasting Committee, he appears rather insulted if you offer him a drink, but then manages to swallow the insult without difficulty.

My Gunnery Officer is living proof that there is no fool like an oiled fool.

At dinner parties, my Flag Lieutenant* talks with more claret than clarity.

Midshipman X has the Principal Medical Officer worried because he has too little blood in his alcohol stream.

Rather timid at work, Flight Lieutenant H soon becomes lion-hearted with the benefit of spirituous liquor, when he will advise his seniors how best to run the squadron, the station – and the Royal Air Force.

The Naval attaché is the nicest chap on two feet, if only he could stay there.

Having attended the Alcohol Rehabilitation course, he has finally succeeded in giving up giving up drinking.

It would appear the only aerobic challenge that this Officer accepts is when hiccupping.

---

* A Royal Navy Admiral's uniformed assistant.

It takes only one drink to make Lieutenant Y drunk, but it is difficult to be sure whether it is the ninth or tenth.

Lieutenant W has been held up several times on his way home, but it was the only way he could get there.

Colonel Q enjoys a workout when he gets up, so he has parallel bars – one for gin and one for brandy.

When this Senior Rate attended the Haslar Alcohol Education Course, his first question concerned the date of the group run-ashore.

COMMON SENSE

I wish this Officer would understand that nought is a mark.

As Navigator's Yeoman he is like a lighthouse in a desert – brilliant but useless.

Flying Officer B is without doubt the most tactless person I have ever met, and we try to keep him away from senior visitors. He could be expected to ask the Prime Minister how much income tax he pays.

Socially, this young helicopter pilot is partial to hell-raising stag parties – but usually knows where to draw the line, or, at worst, who to apologise to the following day.

Furthermore, minor matters such as being four months overdue with library books are not the actions of a high-flying Staff candidate.

In my opinion, this *Sea Harrier* pilot should not be authorised to fly below 250 feet.

My Deputy Weapons Engineer is a 'pickle-jar' Officer. He can tell you the cube root of the surface area of a pickle-jar lid, and to two decimal places at that, but has absolutely no idea how to get the wretched thing off.

This pleasant Cavalry Officer knows he must deploy the 'laid back' approach with care. There is a time and place; falling asleep during the General Officer Commanding's recent address was neither.

His fellow messmates have appointed him as an OSLO – *Outer Space Liaison Officer.*

This Officer Cadet has too much bone in his head and not nearly enough in his spine.

The Deputy Commander always stoops to concur.

Officer Cadet V's initiative knows no bounds – none at all, because it is common sense and judgement that he lacks.

He is a Staff Officer of some conviction, just as soon as he knows what the Admiral thinks.

I don't think that this Midshipman could count past 10 without taking his shoes off.

If there are any original ideas in this candidate's head, they are probably in solitary confinement.

The PT Officer is not very bright, but he can lift heavy weights.

Recruit N has grown up a lot in the past year, and there is some optimism that his IQ* will eventually catch up with his shoe size.

This young Lieutenant is always babbling over with enthusiasm.

The reason that this Officer Cadet has a stupid grin on his face is that – he is stupid.

Midshipman L is a complex fellow who always begins a mystery novel in the middle, so that not only does he not know how it ends, he also doesn't know how it began.

Able Seaman P appeared before me, charged with financial impropriety. In his defence, he stated that there was no way that he could be overdrawn, because he still had twelve cheques in his cheque book.

---

* *Intelligence Quotient – a measure of brain capacity.*

COURAGE AND STAMINA

Lt Col U has high standards, though I have little evidence of any great infatuation with physical fitness.

He has the courage of *her* convictions.

The Senior Engineering Officer believes that only a certain number of heartbeats have been allotted to him, and is reluctant to use any of them up on the sports field.

The Gunnery Officer has had a series of chest infections; he is so full of antibiotics that every time he sneezes, he cures a dozen people.

It would be interesting to know whether this Midshipman has any other ambition in life apart from breathing.

She has her way when they agree, and he has his wife's way when they disagree.

This pleasant Fighter Controller would appear to have a line that makes her rather popular – the line of least resistance.

With regard to hard work, this Able Seaman has a notion – but very little motion.

Private R is as spineless as a cream bun.

I suspect that the only exercise Major G gets is when digging frozen ice trays out of the refrigerator.

EFFECTIVENESS

Even allowing for the fact that this young subaltern is a complete no-hoper, he has had a very poor year.

I am convinced that Officer Cadet D would be out of his depth in a car park puddle.

In spite of the fact that his records show to the contrary, Flying Officer B displays no sign of ever having attended an Officer's Training School.

2nd Lieutenant A has given an unexceptional performance, apart from an outstanding characterisation of a poof in the Unit Pantomime.

Captain Z has fully demonstrated the ability to juggle several of his balls at any one time.

The new Brigadier is so weak and pathetic that he couldn't pull the skin off a rice pudding.

Sub Lieutenant W is such an unco-ordinated shambles that he would have difficulty fighting his way out of a wet paper bag.

The Assistant Caterer's unpolished style was typified by his walking to work with a West Ham United duffel bag slung over his uniform shoulder. His reaction to correction was to obtain an executive briefcase.

This Midshipman has the wisdom of youth, and the energy of old age.

His future looks very secure, as they will probably put him in a strait jacket.

This Instructor needs no introduction; what he really needs is a conclusion.

Sub Lieutenant G is living proof of the adage that if he couldn't take a joke, then he shouldn't have joined.

Petty Officer K knows very little, but knows it very fluently.

I must confess to finding Wing Commander Q's campaign for the betterment and upward progress of Wing Cdr Q a little overpowering. If I was the Pope and Q a Catholic, I should still be concerned about a take-over bid.

Leading Seaman A often lets his mind go blank, but then forgets to turn off the sound.

The Paymaster is so smooth that his friends think they are being cultivated, whereas in fact they are being trimmed.

Pilot Officer H stands out among his brethren because of his size and strength, rather than his personality. The less charitable have suggested that – with the addition of a bolt through the base of his neck – he would be a natural for employment with *Hammer Films*.

Group Captain R is always around when he needs you.

My AdC* has a very special talent for turning opportunities into difficulties.

Despite being warned about his lack of effort as Combat Survival Officer, there has been no improvement in Flight Lieutenant B's conduct. He even arranged a 'wet dinghy' drill for the day following his departure.

Probably the only thing that this young officer has achieved on his own is his dandruff.

Sergeant O claimed an interest in cricket and even had a pair of wicket keeper's gloves. Sadly, the only important thing he caught all summer was chicken pox.

---

*Aide de Campe – traditional (French) term for a military assistant.

As a former Secret Air Service Troop Commander, Major S would see no reason for a mailed fist ever to be delivered inside a velvet glove, except to deaden the sound.

Midshipman G can hardly wait to hear what he is going to say.

To be fair Lieutenant X has only had her present job for four days, but she is already two weeks behind in her work.

Although Petty Officer C has played rugby for the Navy, someone should tell him the difference between pulling his weight and throwing it around.

The way that Sub Lieutenant V handles the truth, he should work for the Met Office.

It is a good thing that Midshipman J does not have to pay taxes on what he thinks he is worth.

I find it surprising that Pilot Officer S, with his known lack of charisma, is going to instructional duties. Such an appointment would only make sense if his new station was a school for the cure of insomnia.

When this Petty Officer was due to depart for a new appointment, the other Senior Rates in his department got together to give him a little momentum.

This Bridge Watchkeeping Officer cannot be paid what he is worth, because it would be below the statutory minimum wage.

This Staff Officer does at least three push-ups every day, from a big leather chair and into the Wardroom for his meals.

The Admiral never passes up a chance to miss business with pleasure.

My Flag Lieutenant thinks that he is a thing of beauty and a boy for ever.

Now that he has reached Air rank he believes that he is as good at attracting women as he never was.

My young lady Doctor is a physiological contradiction. She knows perfectly well that tight clothing stops circulation, yet in her case, the tighter the clothing the more she is in circulation.

In encouraging a woman to tell him about her past, Major F ensures that before she has finished, he has become part of it.

Lots of women may not recall Lieutenant X's name, but his hands are familiar.

Sub Lieutenant A is the sort of chap who, if he fell on his back, would probably cut his chin.

Midshipman S would grace an Edwardian battleship, but little else.

Rather like most of the Peerage, the only thing that this Officer has ever done for a living was to inherit.

Captain L is something of a snob, but he should be less concerned with who he is descended from – and more worried where he is descending to.

Lieutenant Commander G is something of a character actor in that, when he shows any character, he is probably acting.

This Platoon Commander does not demand high standards from himself or his men. He would probably accept an Afghan hound as a guide dog.

Midshipman E's claimed attempts at self-improvement are now on something of a solid foundation. They are on the rocks.

Marine D's ability to work like a horse, but only when cornered like a rat, is an occasional inspiration to those around him.

Corporal N is a charming, sociable and good-looking member of my Ship's Detachment who is very much a model Royal Marine. It is a matter of some regret that he is not a working model.

A quiet North Countryman, Lieutenant Commander F is a *Sea Harrier* fighter pilot of high skill and great modesty. Following an earlier successful combat sortie over Falkland Sound, he described a later patrol as being *"as quiet as an Argentine Air Force crewroom..."*

Private A has tried hard to overcome a number of personal problems, including his difficulties with the telephone. Once he learns to pick up the bone-shaped bit before dialling, and to talk to the end which has the electric string attached, he will probably achieve results.

INTEGRITY

I object to the fact that this Medical Officer has used my ship to carry his genitals from port to port, and the other members of the Wardroom to carry him from bar to bar.

Candidate No. 3 thinks he can push himself forward by patting himself on the back.

Without doubting his motives, I was forced to note that this pilot's dislike for a ground tour manifested itself in a stiff neck which required extensive medical attention. The pain has now gone from his neck, but it remains in mine.

A married man, Lt Colonel F lives in the Mess where he has set a very poor example to the junior officers, particularly by being seen with a woman who is not his wife.

This sailor is something of a contact man – all 'con' and no tact.

Marine B has an interesting financial philosophy. When he borrows money, it is against his principles either to pay interest, or to repay the principal.

If our First Lieutenant had to have his conscience surgically removed, it would be a very minor operation.

The Padre is a small, lithe man who slides about the place in a rather oily fashion.

This potential Royal Marine recruit is a man of several convictions; he has served time for each one.

Lt. Col. K has been baptised by fire in the past, but has now been scorched in the Ministry of Defence.

This man is a phoney; even the wool he tries to pull over your eyes is 50% polyester.

This Padre prays on his knees on Sunday, and preys on everybody else for the rest of the week.

Flying Officer J has straight hair that never lays down properly, small eyes set close together and the startled appearance of a schoolboy caught raiding the tuck shop.

The only reason that 2nd Lieutenant A would get a single vote in a battalion popularity poll is that he would be certain to vote for himself.

The more that Lieutenant C protests his honesty, the more firmly you have to hang onto your wallet.

Should Captain F ever offer to lay his cards on the table, it would be a good idea to count them first.

Pilot Officer K has a flat which I understand he shares with an unmarried lady. He intends to buy the flat, but I am unsure of his intentions towards the lady.

The Welfare Officer has a reputation among the wives for being an advanced member of the Wandering Hands Society.

The less you have to do with him, the less you will be worse off.

Our Sea Cadet Liaison Officer seems too good to be true – and he isn't.

This NCO is the kind of friend who, if you give him a free hand, will stick it straight into your pocket.

As a 'Married Unaccompanied' Officer, Squadron Leader T's social life has been inconsistent with his declared marital status.

Pilot Officer M very much believes in free speech – especially long distance telephone calls from other people's houses.

The Padre's wife belongs to the meddling classes.

Flight Lieutenant N's reputation as a flagrant rule breaker is not really justified, but he does spend a considerable amount of time exploring the borders of legality.

This Young Officer could give failure a bad name.

I have had to put Sub Lieutenant R on Special Report because he is too busy learning the tricks of the trade to learn the trade itself.

For people like him, a friend who isn't in need is his friend indeed.

You can always depend on Sub Lieutenant A to depend on you.

Warrant Officer H has two major faults – nearly everything he says, and almost everything he does.

This officer is a cheerful hypochondriac, in that he very much enjoys bad health.

The science of heredity is what makes parents of children like him wonder about each other.

Four major publishers of fiction are bidding for the rights to this Petty Officer's C.30 Travel Expense claim.

When the PT Officer's conscience bothers him about something that he's done, he will come forward in a very open way and then lie about the whole thing.

You can always tell when the Pusser is lying; if his lips are moving, he is.

Flight Sergeant W tries to whitewash himself by blackening others.

It would be interesting to know on what special experience the CO biases his opinions.

You can often see the Commander smiling when things go wrong – mainly because he's just thought of someone he can blame it on.

This ambitious Supply and Secretarial Officer is a man of firm convictions, just as soon as he knows what everyone above him thinks about the subject.

2nd Lt. O needs to construct a partition between her vivid imagination and the actual facts.

This Officer Candidate is the sort of person who would not hit a man when he is down, but would kick him hard instead.

Commander N always thinks twice before speaking, so that he can come out with something really nasty.

I would advise the Public Relations Officer to buy fire insurance instead of a life policy, because there is no doubt where he is ultimately going.

A suitable motto for this young lady officer's behaviour would be – *'to err is human, but it feels divine...'*

The first recruit stated that he was careful about his health, and that he now only smokes filter-tipped marijuana.

You cannot believe this officer, even when he swears that he is lying.

The only thing that keeps this Senior Rate from being described as a barefaced liar is his beard.

I get the impression that Midshipman X would steal a dead fly from a blind spider.

Look at this Candidate and then at his shoes; you will see three heels.

My Flag Lieutenant has a sunny disposition but a shady past.

The Buffer is so mean that he would throw a drowning man both ends of a rope.

Lieutenant Commander L apparently studied Meteorology so that he could look in a woman's eyes and tell whether.

The Chief Clerk is the sort of man who, if he murdered his parents, would ask for mercy on the grounds that he had recently become an orphan.

This recruit is part of the modern generation who are willing to do an honest day's work, but then want a week's pay for it.

Lieutenant Q was recently caught misappropriating Regimental funds. Claiming a whole range of mitigating circumstances, he threw himself at the mercy of the Court Martial – and missed.

Our Commanding Officer has got about as much conscience as a fox in a chicken coop.

Recruit X suffered a stress fracture of his foot on the assault course last month, and it was healing well until compensationitis set in.

A snap inspection of the Regimental accounts found the Pay Sergeant to be six feet tall and about £5,000 short.

This young Marine is certainly talented, but he appears to regard his time in the Corps as a vacation rather than a vocation.

INTELLIGENCE

As long as his backside points downwards, this young man will never make it as aircrew in the Fleet Air Arm.

This Officer Cadet gives the distinct impression that he has not got both oars in the water.

As an Oxford graduate, Pilot Officer C has a tendency to be condescending to less clever colleagues. I have myself found this trait to be rather irritating.

Midshipman Y is basically a large collection of recessive genes.

My Leading Regulator is not very smart. In fact, he is depriving a police dog of a promising career.

If this young Officer's brains were dynamite, he would not have enough to blow his cap off.

This Parachute Jumping Instructor is a short, thick-set person with practically no neck. His assessments are very much those one would expect from a person of his build.

It is a wonder of neuroscience how such a big head can hold such a tiny mind.

The only reason that Petty Officer G manages to keep his head above water in this appointment is that softwood floats.

There is no doubt that the Postie is a man of rare intelligence, because it's pretty rare for him to show any.

Lieutenant N has a mind which is always on the tip of his tongue.

The Admiralty Interview Board's opinion was that if Candidate E had just a little more sense, he could be described as a half-wit.

Captain T's written work is developing well, as demonstrated by his essay on homosexuality within the British Army.

By retaining this young man in the Royal Navy, we will be depriving an English village of its idiot.

Should this recruit pick up a wooden mallet, two things of equal intelligence would be in close proximity.

The only bone of contention in my Royal Marine advisor's arguments is the bone that lies between his ears.

The reason why Sub Lieutenant R has a chip on his shoulder is that it is sourced from the teak higher up.

The Senior Instructor Officer has an open mind that should now be closed for repairs.

Intellectually, he is such a lightweight that he could tap dance on a chocolate éclair.

This Midshipman is still recovering from an unusual accident which occurred at sea, when a thought suddenly struck him.

It is stretching the imagination enormously to picture Officer Cadet D as the end product of billions of years of evolution.

It would appear that this Officer is listening to his psychiatric advisor and then drawing his own confusions.

This Cadet must be the one person to have a sixth sense, because there is no evidence of the other five.

If ignorance really is bliss, then Officer Cadet F is the world's happiest person.

I have come to the conclusion that Artificer Apprentice Y is even smarter than Professor Stephen Hawking, because only a dozen people understand Hawking, and no one can understand Artificer Apprentice Y.

To be fair, he has demonstrated an admirable coolness and calm when faced with danger, although I would attribute this to a lack of intelligence and imagination.

We have tried very hard, but have now come to the conclusion that it would take a surgical operation to get a thought into Candidate P's head.

I often wonder whether this Troop Commander is smoking something unusual, because he has that certain nothing when it comes to creative ideas.

Officer Cadet J is not just an ordinary moron, he is the *moron's* moron.

I understand from the psychiatrists that he is totally psycho-ceramic – a genuine crackpot.

One always senses that there are a few cogs missing from the Adjutant's intellectual gearbox.

The final candidate, Ms. WOODHEAD, was most aptly named.

Miss B has a mind like concrete – all mixed up and permanently set.

LEADERSHIP

The Assistant Quartermaster will not set the world on fire; if by chance, he did, he certainly would not be able to put it out.

His men would follow him anywhere, but only out of curiosity.

You cannot help admiring the Commodore, because if you don't, he'll sack you.

Sergeant N has many of the attributes of a natural leader combined with a vigorous personality. However, his followers soon reduce in number as they realise the rather erratic nature of the course on which they are set.

Flight Lieutenant W confuses aircraft captaincy with the incantation of meaningless phraseology.

Rear Admiral P always tells his staff that even if it is only a suggestion, they should never forget who is actually making it.

Colonel R usually talks of principle, but tends to act entirely on self-interest.

Should the Boss pat you on the back, he is probably working out just where to stick the knife in.

This Head of Department is the sort of chap who likes to eat his cake and have yours too.

The First Lieutenant is a strong supporter of law and order, but only if he can lay down the law – and then give the orders.

If the Commandant wants your opinion he will most certainly give it to you.

Air Commodore W is leading his staff on such a rat race that they are on strike for more cheese.

Captain Z has a difficulty for every solution.

Our new Midshipman is so insignificant that he could get lost in a crowd of two.

This Cadet serves one most useful purpose in life, in that he is a horrible example to everyone else.

I can recall Pilot Officer M's father as being a remote, mean bastard; his son is a chip off the old glacier.

If this RAF Regiment Officer was a little more laid back, he would be supine.

I have to report that Squadron Leader H is the last sort of chap we should have involved in the training of our young men, even Navigators.

As Chief-of-Staff he has a perfect way of ending meetings; he tells all those opposed to his plan that they can resign.

There are so many 'yes men' on his staff that the Headquarters has been nicknamed *The Land of Nod*.

Midshipman H is as spineless as a length of wet spaghetti.

Success has not changed this Commanding Officer one bit; he is still the same stinker that he always was.

As far as Leading Seaman T is concerned, a friend in need is a friend to stay away from.

You can be certain that 2nd Lieutenant F will never get dizzy from doing a good turn.

This General List Seaman Officer is so controlled, and so tight, that he is unable to perspire freely.

With a little more effort on this Cadet's part, he could become a total non-entity.

Flying Officer A possesses all the qualities one would expect in a Captain – of a pirate ship.

Although highly competent in submarine matters, he is a rather lazy Executive Officer. With his excellent powers of delegation, he would be far better suited for Command.

When put under pressure, her voice rises to a pitch that can only be understood by bats.

Having heard much about him, I had hoped that Lt Cdr B would not live up to his reputation, but sadly, I have been disappointed.

Some Divisional Commanders are born great, while others achieve greatness by their actions; this one has a Public Relations Officer.

ORGANIZATION / MANAGEMENT ABILITY

Able Seaman B was once a farmhand; he should return to an agricultural career as soon as possible.

Our Instructor Officer is somewhat disorganised and has three pairs of spectacles. One is for near sight, the second for far sight, and the third to look for either of the other two.

Wing Commander V is really not so much of a 'has-been', but more of a definitely 'won't-be'.

As Officer of the Watch, he has carried out each and every one of his duties to his entire satisfaction.

Lieutenant Colonel P recently retired from the Army under something of a cloud. He has now returned as a civilian contractor, proving that those that can – do, but those that can't – become consultants.

The only job that this young recruit has any interest in, and is ideally qualified for, is as a tester in a mattress factory.

Her interests have been broadened since she married a *Phantom* pilot.

If hedonism was a religion, my Medical Officer would be its high priest.

Since my last report Pilot Officer J has reached rock bottom, and has now started to dig.

The Company second-in-command is somewhat wrapped up in himself, but it all makes for a pretty small parcel.

Not given to displays of enthusiasm nor an energetic man, Squadron Leader S ponders at length over problems. I suspect that if he discovered a fire, by the time he had called the Fire Brigade, the blaze would have burned out.

People and things are here today and gone tomorrow, but the Commander is always here today – and here tomorrow.

It is uncertain what this Navigator's future will be, mainly because this will involve the Medical Branch having to make a decision.

As a child it would appear that Sub Lieutenant W wanted to be a Supply Officer badly. He has now achieved his ambition, because he is a bad Supply Officer.

Chief Petty Officer R is running a large scale operation, but with a small scale mind.

I agree that Lieutenant Commander C, when faced with a problem, usually stops to think, but unfortunately he then forgets to start again.

Leading Seaman R has not got many faults, but he certainly makes the most of the ones he has.

The only time that my Navigating Officer is absolutely certain of where he is going is shortly after he has taken a laxative.

They say that the Civilian Administrative Officer's deputy kisses the boss's feet every day. This is not actually true, because his boss doesn't come to work every day.

Lieutenant Commander H appears to think that he is indispensable to the organization, but a pair of shoe trees could do a better job at filling the appointment than he does.

This Admiralty Interview Board candidate will never be interested in teamwork; it appears that all his life he has followed the path of least assistance.

My Supply Officer is always ready to help you get what is coming to him.

The new Training Officer has been accurately described as a 'big thinker', but by someone who lisps.

There is so much unhappiness in his Department that it is frequently closed for altercations.

My Supply Officer is the sort of pessimist who always turns out the light to see how dark it is.

During her Naval career, Wren B-Z moved in the best triangles.

It would appear that before he joined the Navy, this young stoker paid his taxes with a smile; the Inland Revenue are now after him for the money.

This Formation Commander has now recommended all three of his COs for promotion to General – which probably explains why he will never get there himself.

Although no flyer, this REME* Officer is a very sound aircraft engineer.

When unsure of himself, this young officer mumbles; when in trouble, he delegates. In a peacetime Navy, he will probably go all the way to the top.

---

* *Royal Electrical and Mechanical Engineers.*

There was a crisis at Command HQ last week when the mainframe computer failed, and – for a change – all the Staff Officers had to think for themselves.

Along with my Budget Control officer, I find the MOD's new financial management strategy tedious in the extreme. Just as we manage to make both ends meet, some cretin in Whitehall then moves the ends.

The computerisation of our Directorate is not going well. The building is full of consultants who say they are solving problems that we didn't know we had, and doing so in a way that we cannot understand.

PERSONAL QUALITIES

As the sole Brit working in NATO Headquarters, Lt Col X bore the shame of not being American with dignity and patience, while the monosyllabic 'Forrest Gump lookalikes' jockeyed for position and influence around him.

Even though he comes from a long line of fellow Hussars, I would not breed from this Officer.

At all times the Station Adjutant is ably assisted by his wife, although I do wish she would acquire the art of selecting the correct dress for an occasion.

Pilot Officer J needs to have his corners rounded off.

This Special Duties Officer is technically sound, but socially impossible.

He is a Northumbrian with a very open personality and no hint of affectation or guile. He is therefore not a natural candidate for AdC duties.

My Assistant Secretary sets low personal standards, and then consistently fails to achieve them.

Personal hygiene is not this subaltern's strongest suit. In fact, he smells like a zoo-keeper's boot.

Flight Lieutenant S has been a highly competent and popular Chairman of the Station Theatre Club, where his powers of persuasion extended to getting no less than four wing commanders to play (in turn) the back legs of a pantomime horse.

Major Z rather epitomises the popular *Royal Greenjacket* image – exceptionally bright, highly intelligent, ambitious, confident – and rather arrogant.

This WRAF* Officer has turned out to be more elegant than useful.

There is reason to be sorry for those who have to work with this man. In general, life is what you make it, but then Sergeant E comes along and makes it worse.

Physically weak, she is rather like warm beer – and is similarly flat.

---

* *Women's Royal Air Force.*

Lieutenant O was decorated after the Falklands War, but success turned his head and left him facing in the wrong direction.

Leading Wren A is so fond of the chaps that her legs are putting in for Separation Pay.

The Search and Rescue Flight Commander has a dark and almost swarthy appearance, and when he lets his hair get out of control he resembles a Mexican bandit.

Lieutenant Commander D is a tall, thin, bearded and very smart officer with the cultivated aura of a rather dangerous gangster.

The only disturbing character trait is his affection for a tarantula spider that he keeps in his office.

I am told that our Nursing Sister is something of a flower that grows wild in the woods.

This student's flying was interrupted for two months by a car crash which very much confirmed him as a 'middle-of-the-road' character.

The Senior Observer's primary interest means that he can only count up to sex.

There is nothing that Midshipman D would not do for a friend, and he intends to keep it that way.

Major R is eccentric; he does not wear socks, and also dresses like Lawrence of Arabia.

Lieutenant X has gone the way of all flash.

Commander P is so conceited that he ordered his ID card photograph to be retouched.

Squadron Leader Q has a large moustache, a large waistline and a matching opinion of himself.

The Provost Sergeant's armpits have been compared less favourably to the interior of a Sumo wrestler's jockstrap.

I think that 2nd Lieutenant B's inflated ego is Mother Nature's compensation for her mediocrity.

He considers himself to be a self-made man, but he would have done better if he had let out the contract.

If this recruit was to be reincarnated in an appropriate form, we would suggest that he comes back as a toad.

How this chap ever gained a Queen's Commission will remain one of life's great mysteries. If it were not for his uniform, I would judge him to be of Junior NCO rank in both manner and appearance.

Squadron Leader V's financial problems seem to stem from the fact that he was once a prolific sower of wild oats. He is now finding the harvesting fees rather expensive.

The Colonel tends to deprive you of privacy without providing any sort of company.

My Medical Officer is a lively officer with style, and has matured well over the past year – even though he does own some terrible bow ties.

Midshipman D's swollen head is merely Mother Nature's attempt to fill a vacuum.

For what it's worth, my wife also reports well on his qualities.

As Lieutenant X's host, you wish he would leave and let live.

I believe that I could cope with Squadron Leader Smith – as long as Mrs Smith was posted.

It is amazing how the Senior Dental Surgeon manages to enter a room voice first.

Lieutenant Cdr J speaks eight languages, but cannot hold his tongue in one.

The Operations Officer's usual comment is a guffaw, and his proclivity for social solecisms like nose-picking and hair-combing are unrestrained by any sense of occasion. Even in an increasingly permissive society, I cannot see him being promoted.

Pilot Officer L has a superiority complex for no good reason.

The Supply Officer (Cash) is oilier than the *Torrey Canyon*.

Warrant Officer M's cheerful demeanour overrides hardship, and he is caring without being patronising. It is therefore surprising that he is also well liked and supported by his superiors.

It is a source of wonderment that – while exercise is supposed to eliminate fat – Miss S still has a double chin.

In fairness, our Catering Officer is doing his best and does not look obese – rather he appears to be about a foot short in stature.

The Support Flight Commander has an attractive, vivacious, trouble-making wife.

This Supply and Secretariat Officer should become a Socialist politician. He doesn't just sit on the fence – he changes sides more often than a windscreen wiper.

It comes as a continuing surprise to me that C is still numbered among the officers of the Royal Air Force.

When Major C was growing up, his main ambition was to be a pirate, and it's not everyone that can realise their ambition in the way that he has.

Lt Cdr M very much believes in the greatest good for the greatest number, but his idea of the greatest number is 'Number One'.

The Senior Pilot never forgets a favour, just as long as he did it.

Every morning the Captain's wife carries out two vital actions – she brushes her teeth and then sharpens her tongue.

I have advised Leading Seaman V that, if they ever put a price on his head, he would be well advised to take it.

When she took a leading part in the Station play, the Air Staff Officer's performance had a very happy ending when the curtain finally came down.

Commander P has risen from obscurity – and is headed for oblivion.

Sub Lieutenant N has only three failings in his drive for the top, namely a gross shortage of talent, a complete lack of ambition, and a total absence of initiative.

My initial impressions of Cadet A were not favourable; he is overweight and gives the impression that *'manana'* is far too urgent a concept for him.

Midshipman J will always remember what he gives – but then forget what he receives.

Pilot Officer M's only saving grace is that he does not mean to be an oaf – he just is one.

I understand that Ms G's present difficulties result from an incident when someone offered her a couple of drinks in his flat – and she reclined.

Leading Seaman C sent his photograph to a Lonely Hearts Club, but they replied that they weren't that lonely.

The Senior Metereology Officer has all the dynamic personality of the side wall of a deserted squash court.

Although unmarried and an Old Harrovian, Flying Officer P is not a contender for an AdC appointment. He is much too big, is not very good at writing letters – and he would be very expensive to feed.

The Padre's life is so dull that he actually looks forward to dental appointments.

The Commodore is unhappily unmarried.

This Physical Education Specialist is a stupid officer; I only wish that his intellect was a tenth of his body strength.

Officer Cadets like him make you wish that birth control was retrospective.

Earlier in his career Major B was told to be himself, but could not have been given worse advice.

Able Seaman A has, like everyone else, the right to have some faults. Sadly, he makes the most of the ones he has, and totally abuses that privilege.

Our Medical Officer is something of a manic depressive – easy glum, easy glow.

The Padre is so narrow-minded that he has to stack his ideas vertically.

The Confidential Books Officer is such a pain in the neck that the people who make *Brufen* pay him a royalty.

Flight Lieutenant H fades entirely into the wallpaper. Since he cannot organise the Squadron silver properly, I am pretty sure he could not look after Air Force 'Brass'* either. He is totally unsuitable for AdC duties.

There is no middle ground where this Staff Officer is concerned; you either hate him or detest him.

In evolutionary terms, Colour Sergeant L is on the return trip.

The only person who drinks more beer in the Mess than this officer is his wife.

---

* *Slang term for Senior Officers with heavily gilded caps.*

It is likely that if he dies, most people would attend the Director's funeral to be absolutely sure that he was dead.

Our Brigadier is the sort of person who reads the obituary notices to cheer himself up.

The First Lieutenant's new glasses have helped his vision, but without changing his point of view.

This Warrant Officer has not been himself lately, and everyone hopes he will stay that way.

At ship's cocktail parties the Weapons Engineering Officer has a surefire way of handling temptation – he yields to it.

In social terms the Air Commodore is still embarrassed at having been born in a bed – with a woman.

There is no point of telling this young Trainee a joke with a double meaning, because he won't get either of them.

This Midshipman is so lazy that he won't even exercise discretion.

Wing Commander Y is a very personable officer who could charm the warts off a frog.

This SD Officer candidate's style of soft sell would be more successful if he was given the right vehicle for his talents, namely an ice cream van.

At the ship's Christmas Concert, his talents as an entertainer could best be described as half-comedian, and half-wit.

This SD* Officer claims that he is self-made, but it's a pity that he left out the working parts.

She has very little willpower, and even less won't power.

This young man has had to give up one bad habit on joining the Royal Marines, and he no longer smokes pot while playing poker.

One young recruit was so tough that he was awarded a scholarship to Borstal.

There is nothing complex about this retired Womens Royal Naval Service Officer, since anyone can grasp her.

This Supply Officer (Cash) can always be counted on to do the right thing too late, or the wrong thing too soon.

Special Duties (RN) – Commissioned from the ranks.

This Officer Cadet's idea of social refinement is to wear a T-shirt when serving tea.

Squadron Leader C's table manners need improvement; when he is taking soup, the noise is similar to an elephant seal dragging itself up onto a beach.

I understand that Lieutenant Colonel B was bitten by an adder, and that it was a terrible sight watching the poor snake curl up and die.

There must be a lot of good left in this retired Officer, but none of it ever comes out.

A chunky individual, the Signals Officer is an ardent sportsman, though modest in both manoeuvrability and stopping distance.

If Lieutenant Commander A were to swim through shark-infested waters he would survive, thanks to professional courtesy.

This young MoD* Desk Officer appears to be frank and earnest with women. I understand that in London he is Frank, while in Portsmouth he is Ernest.

Although this Medical Services Officer is hoping to settle down eventually, his social behaviour indicates little life expectancy.

* *Ministry of Defence.*

This young woman is a lover of the outdoors, but doesn't do too badly indoors either.

Her taste in the opposite sex has a very uniform quality – sailors and Royal Marines.

Candidates like Mr X do not grow on trees, they swing from them.

When Lieutenant N goes on a run ashore he has plenty of *savoir-faire*, but never the taxi fare.

Lance Corporal I is the sort of chap who cannot be ordered around, unless it is a round of drinks.

If the First Lieutenant ever took a £5 note out of his pocket, the figurehead of the Queen would start blinking in the light.

The Brigade Major is so cold blooded that, if a mosquito bit him, it would die from pneumonia.

Every organization is supposed to cherish its eccentrics, but I find this difficult in the case of Major B; his moustache is too long, and his hair is too short.

It is quite difficult to know what makes this experienced Submariner tick, but nearly impossible to understand what also makes him chime on the hour.

The majority of his Royal Marines Officer batch are liked wherever they go, but he is only liked whenever he goes.

As a dedicated fisherman, he has the kind of temperament that goes with a person who finds a night on a cold and windy beach to be a stimulating experience.

A suitable finishing touch to this candidate's report would have been a *Swan Vesta* match.

The members of this new Young Officer intake are alike in many disrespects.

The only thing that Flight Lieutenant Z will share with you willingly is a communicable disease.

Colour Sergeant X is the sort of man who would knife you in the back – and then promptly report you for carrying concealed weapons.

As I write this, Spring is very much in the air, but not in Warrant Officer J.

Give Chief Petty Officer Q an inch – and he will measure it.

This young lady Officer recently met a man in the strangest way – they were introduced.

My WRAC* driver should learn some other four letter words like *"can't"*, *"stop"* and *"don't"*.

Petty Officer X's private life is a bed of ruses.

This Officer is tall, dark and hands.

The Senior Pilot has not let a woman pin anything on him since he was a baby.

The Deputy WEO** has dirty fingernails, and a mind to match.

Sub Lieutenant Q is never troubled by improper thoughts; in fact he enjoys them very much.

This Officer Cadet appears to think that the world owes him a giving.

Although the Executive Officer always tries to get something for nothing, he'll readily complain about quality of service.

Should Commander U ever pay you a compliment, he will then ask for a receipt.

This senior female Officer is in the prim of life.

His appearance indicates many years on hard stations but good rations.

---

* Women's Royal Army Corps.
** Weapons Engineering Officer.

Warrant Officer M never gets the 'flu because no self-respecting virus could stand him.

She is so unpleasant that the chap who took her out recently got a certificate from the Royal Humane Society.

If Moses had actually met the Regimental Sergeant Major, I'm sure there would have been another Commandment.

My impression is that the less he knows, the more stubbornly he knows it.

This Admiral's son failed to impress the Board; he is so conceited as to be almost useless.

Uneducated, ungrateful, unforgettable – and unfortunately mine.

I had many doubts about the principle of re-incarnation until I encountered this young man; his *alter ego* is Walter Mitty.

From the tailoring point of view, this Lieutenant is a complete shambles. His uniform jacket only fits where it touches, and his peaked cap looks as if it has just crash-landed on his head.

I note that this Officer Candidate was born on the 2nd of April, just one day too late.

Petty Officer L continues to get in and out of the most awful scrapes. He tells me that he has just met the most beautiful woman in the world; unfortunately, her husband wants her back.

The teaching staff have been struggling to establish a reason for Officer Cadet B's existence; we think that he is here to remind us that not everything in Nature's grand design has a sensible purpose.

This Staff Officer is moving on after three years. We are pleased to be regaining his car parking slot.

This Petty Officer is living proof of the old adage that any fool can criticise – and many of them do.

Despite constant advice and support from the Regimental medical section, Lance Corporal W's idea of a balanced diet is to have a bacon butty* in each hand.

This Staff Officer would definitely improve if he laughed at himself once in a while. Everyone else does.

Major B has a resigned look on his face most of the time; I only wish that he would put it in writing.

---

* Slang term for a sandwich.

This Admiralty Interview Board candidate was conceited beyond belief. It appears that his main reason for joining the Royal Navy was so that the world could see him.

Our Physical Training Instructor is so vain that he is reluctant to take a hot shower in case the bathroom mirror steams up.

When the Principal Medical Officer was selected for promotion, his acute proctoheliosis became a chronic condition. The sun now shines from his backside all day.

This young man cannot see the connection between getting up in the morning and getting on in the Army.

Corporal D claims that there is Royalty amongst his ancestors. Judging by his build and speech, one of those ancestors must have been *King Kong*.

The Air Marshal is a hatchet-faced martinet who appears to have had a charisma bypass very early in his career.

Recruit X was skinny, weak and hopelessly underconfident when he joined the Army. He then failed to capitalise on these natural assets.

POWER OF EXPRESSION

Lt. Commander J adopts a rather tangential approach to problems, deftly side-stepping the main issues to arrive at a conclusion which bears little or no relation to the original difficulty.

The Mess Manager regularly appears in theatrical productions – both on the stage and off.

Officer Cadet V speaks no foreign languages and even has difficulty with English; he tends to communicate in grunts.

The Admiral's wife loves wordy causes.

As a decision maker, Commander S is a master of the 'definite maybe' and of the 'positive perhaps'.

When Sub Lieutenant V opens her mouth, it is only to change whichever foot was previously in there.

In speech, the Deputy Chief of Staff tends to be rather long-winded, and insists on continuing his involved arguments even when his subject agrees with him; Commander K will simply not take 'yes' for an answer.

My AdC must learn to resist the temptation to produce the right answer instantly; most of the time he cannot wait to hear what he is going to say next.

When there is nothing more to be said, Lt Cdr I is still saying it.

2nd Lieutenant J has both a diarrhoea of words and a constipation of ideas.

Miss Q never opens her mouth unless she has nothing to say.

When all is said and done, Captain O just keeps on talking.

This Flight Lieutenant's vocabulary is rather small, but the turnover is terrific.

This Officer Cadet would be that much better off if his mind could work as fast as his mouth.

The Supply Officer has an oily tongue to go with his slick mind.

In conversation, this young Midshipman would do well to follow the example of his skull shape, and come to the point early.

Our Welfare Wren Petty Officer is the sort of person whose word is never done.

If Lieutenant H ever said what he thought, he would suddenly become speechless.

Lieutenant Commander X can talk 50% faster than anyone can listen.

The smaller Petty Officer J's ideas are, the more words he uses to express them.

Any attempts at insight into Officer Cadet G's religious beliefs have floundered on the rock of incoherence.

Commander Y is the sort of chap who would take two hours to tell you that he is a man of few words.

This talkative officer should be on an allowance of 300 words a day.

I cannot understand how this Intelligence Corps Officer has reached the SO2 grade; my Chief of Staff confirms that he holds the record for *'I don't knows'* at briefings so far this year.

No one is the Flight Commander's equal at using more words to say less about nothing.

Lieutenant Y can be relied upon to contribute more heat than light to a discussion.

The claim that new technology has developed a fog which can be made to order is no news to this young man.

The First Lieutenant's stories tend to have a happy ending, mainly because his listeners are delighted when they finally end.

This Officer Cadet is a young man of few words; the trouble is that he keeps repeating them.

If the room sudenly falls silent, you can safely conclude that Midshipman G has just told a joke.

The Training Major is such a motormouth that he could talk a glass eye to sleep.

Lieutenant Commander T is a Grandmaster of the inappropriate remark.

The Adjutant always speaks straight from the shoulder; most unfortunately, some of his comments do not appear to start from higher up.

You like Midshipman X a lot when you first meet him, but he will soon talk you out of that.

His lecturing technique is absolutely hypnotic.

This Instructor Officer's teaching technique is described as akin to a bicycle wheel; the longer the spoke, the greater the tyre.

He can be highly lucid and creative on paper, but verbal exchange is lethal for anyone seeking a straightforward and useful answer.

This Staff College student shows great potential. Ask him what the time is, and he will tell you how his watch works, in extraordinary detail.

Midshipman E's communication skills are something of a lottery; he is usually on a different planet to those around him, and one can never be certain that he has understood a given task.

This candidate's last Staff College essay was well received by all his tutors, mainly because they hoped that it really was.

The Chaplain charges nothing for his sermons; this is terrific value for money.

Our CO is a devout Christian who only uttered two swear words during his three year tenure. One was an adjective, the other a noun; both were directed at the Padre, who was still skulking in the bottom of a trench some hours after the air raid had passed.

I think Lieutenant R shows great promise as an Instructor, because he has that critical ability to impart knowledge without possessing any.

Major P has achieved an Open University degree in Sociology that has changed him noticeably; his staff work is now full of the kind of jargon which is totally incomprehensible.

PROFESSIONAL KNOWLEDGE

Some eight months ago I forecast an improvement in this Aircrew Officer's performance, once he became operational. Regrettably, he then crashed his aircraft into the sea.

When this student pilot lifts his helicopter into the hover, he initiates a sequence of events over which he appears to have very little subsequent control.

Sub Lieutenant B is a big gun of small calibre and immense bore.

My Principal Medical Officer claims to be a GP, but he is so full of himself that he is regarded by his staff as something of an 'I' Specialist.

It's not so much that Sub Lieutenant D lacks presence of mind when conducting his bridge duties; the problem lies more with a total absence of thought.

On a recent progress test this Artificer candidate not only got every answer wrong, but he also mis-spelled his name.

Flying Officer E is now just safe enough to be entrusted with the aircraft while the captain attends to the call of nature. We try not to crew him with captains with weak bladders.

When asked what she thought about Red China, this potential Officer said that it was acceptable as long as it did not clash with the tablecloth.

The Naval attaché is the sort of diplomat who can speak for an hour without notes – and without a point.

To paraphrase Charles Dickens, the Adjutant's expenditure of words is far too great for his income of ideas.

Flying Officer S is holder of the bedding inventory of the Mess. He recently married a WRAF* Officer.

This young Surgeon Lieutenant handles the nurses to good effect.

He has decided to learn the trombone, I think, because it is an instrument with which you can succeed by letting things slide.

---

* Women's Royal Air Force.

Sub Lieutenant F's conceit is in an inverse relationship to his lack of ability.

My Correspondence Officer could talk the hind leg off a donkey, and is in no way embarrassed by knowing nothing about the subject he is discussing.

My secretary appears to have been hired on the basis of glamour, rather than grammar.

We were disturbed to find that this student pilot was intending to leave in the near future, because we had hoped that he would have left by the end of this week.

This Instructor Officer intends to become an author and has just finished something which was accepted by a writer's magazine – the application form for a year's subscription.

In the matter of seduction our CO is always ready, villain and able.

Sub Lieutenant the Honourable Quentin F-J has been borne for watchkeeping duties; his family may be listed in *Who's Who*, but he certainly doesn't know what's what.

This Dental Officer has been filling in.

This student's overall performance has confirmed that he ceased to develop intellectually at a relatively early age, and that he will always remain oblivious to the consequences of his invariably crass and stupid behaviour. He was formally counselled by me regarding his specific shortcomings and low assessments; his reaction was that he thought he had better join the Royal Australian Air Force.

The Observer thinks he knows it all, and then keeps proving that he doesn't.

It is a constant source of amusement that this pilot's handling of the *Hawk* aircraft befits one who has an agricultural degree.

Lieutenant Commander M remains optimistic about his career, but in this matter he stands alone.

I have yet to fly with this Pilot Officer, but having seen him pull up the aircraft steps in an outward display of efficiency before his Navigator had even climbed aboard, I am not exactly looking forward to the experience.

The PT Officer's contribution to the Station's water-saving policy was to suggest closing two lanes of the gymnasium swimming pool.

I do not think that we can retain this young man in the Royal Navy. Following a ten minute 'stand easy', he has to be retrained.

My Chief Petty Officer was sent on a three month attachment to learn the Norwegian language. His post-course report concludes that he now speaks Norwegian like a native – of Turkey.

My Medical Officer is a pessimist who ought to specialise in venereology; he describes life as a 'sexually transmitted disease that is invariably fatal..'

In matters of sonar technology, Sub Lieutenant M behaves as if he has a lifetime's experience; in reality, he is hardly out of the egg.

My Medical Officer defines an alcoholic as someone who drinks more than his doctor. We have no alcoholics in my ship.

The Senior armoured warfare instructor is getting a little staid. Some of his teaching stems from a time when the word *Centurion* meant rank, not a tank.

RELIABILITY

Pilot Officer C is certainly very fit, and smashes tiles and bricks with either foot or hand.

This young lady has delusions of adequacy.

Wing Commander A's final exit was true to form in that he failed to appear at a farewell luncheon arranged on his behalf.

As a work colleague, Flight Sergeant D is long on promises but short on memory.

Real talent, totally reliable – and Cambridge-educated too!

When Lieutenant Commander L wishes you 'Good morning', it would be a wise precaution to check this with the Met Office.

This Sub Lieutenant is somewhat highly strung; unfortunately, he has not been strung high enough.

There are many who consider that the programme runs a lot better on the Chief Instructor's day off.

This Commanding Officer will only face the music if he can call the tune.

His Department bought him an appropriate gift. It was both timely and striking – a carriage clock.

There is a lot less to this Officer than meets the eye.

I must admit to liking Capt E, particularly as he has the good taste to be the only other officer in the Brigade who supports Queen's Park Rangers.

It would not be possible to describe this Administrative Officer as a quitter, because he has been sacked from every appointment that he has ever had.

This former actor is something of a dandy who has long been waiting for something to turn up. Flight Lieutenant V should have started with his own shirt sleeves.

I have been asked to write Lieutenant W a satisfactory letter of reference. Lieutenant W worked for us for a year, but is no longer working for us. We are very satisfied.

Midshipman Y is a most dependable person, because you can always depend on him to get it completely wrong.

As a Part of Ship officer in my frigate, Lieutenant A has been almost invisible.

He remains overweight, scruffy and very noisy. These faults might not be so bad if he was a member of the Stoker's messdeck, but in a Leading Steward they are unacceptable.

Fat, untidy and cantankerous, Warrant Officer S maintains a wide range of interests outside the Service. He is a man of narrow views and limited reliability; on current form he just about deserves to remain employed until the end of the week.

Delightful, delinquent but potentially disastrous; he should not be allowed anywhere near real soldiers and live ammunition.

2nd Lieutenant X's attitude to planning is that if you don't bother, it saves you a lot of work and worry and, as a bonus, failure comes as no surprise.

This applicant for a replacement South Atlantic Medal claims to have been in the 1982 Falklands campaign, but we suspect the only war record that he has is *Brothers in Arms* by Mark Knopfler and Dire Straits.

TACT & CO-OPERATION

This officer should go far – and the sooner he starts, the better.

His wife, who is anti-social and ill-mannered, fortunately refuses to take part in any Air Station functions.

Major F regards free speech not as a right, but as a continuous obligation.

When the war starts, this young man will end up with a chest full of silver. If captured, he will make life hell for the prison camp commandant; until then, he continues to practise on me.

As guests go, you wish he would.

The Padre can stay longer for an hour than most people do for a week.

Commander (Training) has a wide circle of nodding acquaintances.

Sub Lieutenant P not only encroaches on your time, he trespasses on eternity.

Midshipman K leaves little to your imagination, and even less to your patience.

Flight Lieutenant Z is a character. He has a lively Cockney turn of phrase, a well developed sense of the ridiculous, and is much liked by everyone. His suitability for an exchange tour is very much a matter of taste; the Australians would like him, but I am not sure about the Americans.

My Flag Lieutenant can talk for hours about the value of silence.

This Administrative expert is exceptionally well supported by his charming and attractive wife, who has an excellent future in the Royal Air Force.

Commander B stands for everything that he thinks I will fall for.

Supervising this officer is like serving on a bomb disposal unit – one is never sure when he is going to go off.

The only time this young woman will listen to an argument is when her colleagues are having a go at each other.

This Senior Rating has been described as a 'grumpy bear'; he is more like a consumptive porcupine with ingrowing quills.

This Petty Officer thinks that the world is against him, and what's more – he is right.

This aircrew Pilot Officer is a punchy little chap with an awkward and supercilious manner. His attitude makes him a walking advertisement for the campaign to bring back Sergeant pilots.

Lieutenant F joined my ship as something of a blue-eyed boy. I have found him to be so full of bullshit that the eye colour on his ID card should be changed to 'brown'.

The Captain's Secretary is the sort of chap who will roll out the carpet for you one day, and then pull it out from under you the next.

Warrant Officer X is a genius, because he not only takes infinite pains in what he is doing, he also gives the same.

Is this candidate a direct descendant of *Attilla the Hun?*

He is an unpleasant, irritating, offensive and obnoxious individual – and these are his good points.

It is to be hoped that one day Sub Lieutenant W may come forth with a few brilliant flashes of silence.

The Base Supply Officer is ably supported by his wife, who is a great exponent of the appealing art of décolletage.

Since his last report, Sub Lieutenant W's personal situation has improved, from his own point of view, in two basic ways: he has ditched his wife, and acquired a desirable car.

Officer Cadet E closely resembles a *Teenage Mutant Ninja Turtle*.

Warrant Officer Q is the sort of man who makes you wish that you had a hearing aid – so that you could turn it off and shut him out.

The Commander's Assistant is so unpleasant that the last time he was in the Royal Hospital Haslar, he even got 'Get Well' cards from the nurses.

I hope that Flight Lieutenant B sorts himself out; there is potential in there somewhere. I would not see him as an AdC, other than to an Air Officer who has a low blood pressure problem.

Flight Lieutenant K has requested an exchange tour in the USA; posting this officer to America would be akin to restoring the tax on tea.

I dislike this Officer's attitude to his superiors; it would appear that his motto for success is that it isn't who you know that matters, but who you 'yes'.

We will probably have difficulties with this young recruit; when he was at school he made his teacher stay in after work.

Brigadier C is the sort of chap who will tell a woman that her tights are wrinkled, even when she is not wearing any.

If getting up people's noses was a prerequisite for promotion, Pilot Officer F would be an Air Commodore by now.

Should this young Officer Cadet live long enough to become an adult, it will be a remarkable tribute to his instructors' self control.

Everyone has a good word for the Commander, but they tend to whisper it.

You can rely on Sub Lieutenant B to tell a woman that she is a sight instead of a vision.

The sparks certainly fly when this young lady uses a knife and fork.

The Mess Caterer continues to be a reliable social chameleon; he is able to blend into the current mood, no matter how raucous the occasion.

The ship's Flight Commander is only dull and uninteresting until you get know him; then he is just plain boring.

Sub Lieutenant B is good for people's health, because when they see him coming they tend to go for long walks.

Socially this Navigator is temperate and, on first acquaintance, quite likeable. However, he soon becomes a boor and is unpopular with his subordinates, his colleagues – and me.

This impertinent youth not only explains everything, but he also then explains his explanations.

Corporal P is basically a good man, even if there are still some dinosaur genes lurking.

I could not warm to this Officer even if we were cremated together.

The senior lady Officer has a laugh like the screech of a rusty door.

When Major L slaps you on the back, it is to make sure that you swallow what he has just told you.

Some people are born great, some become great; Commander G just grates.

In short, he is one step ahead of notoriety and two steps astern of fame.

The Assistant Adjutant should be kept away from official cocktail parties; she is the human equivalent of a social hand grenade.

This local landowner is a bit eccentric, but essentially harmless; a claim that an ancestor fell at Waterloo is true. His great grandfather slipped off the platform.

This bright young REME Major recently graduated from Staff College. He is smart enough to tell me exactly how to run my business, but not smart enough to realise that, in the current atmosphere of Force reductions, I could ask him to start one of his own – as a civilian.

The belligerence displayed by this young Sandhurst Officer Cadet will be difficult to contain. If he was ever ordered to bury the hatchet, he would do so in the middle of a nearby forehead.

When seniority is combined with arrogance, advice is even less welcome than usual; Squadron Leader P needs it the most – but likes it the least.

The General is the sort of man who says he welcomes an exchange of opinions, but whichever one you arrive with, he will tell you to go away with his.

ZEAL AND INITIATIVE

Flying Officer P reminds me very much of a gyroscope; he is always spinning around at a frantic pace, but in reality not going anywhere at all.

When he joined my ship, this Special Duties Lieutenant was something of a granny, but since then he has aged considerably.

Midshipman L is the type of person who approaches every subject with an open mouth.

Flight Lieutenant L is a real trier who nearly knocks his cap off every time he salutes.

A long standing middle-of-the-road officer, Squadron Leader G is now grinding to a halt at the kerbside, and has taken the cul-de-sac of voluntary redundancy.

Second Lieutenant K is a highly-polished chap, but in a slippery sort of way.

In both attitude and commitment, Able Seaman P resembles a slug on an ice rink.

This *Royal Fusilier* subaltern reminds one of a slightly unruly colt that needs schooling to bring out the best.

Flight Lieutenant E rarely sets the crewroom on fire, and not just because he has given up smoking.

As Squadron Adjutant he is the personification of keenness without actually being very useful.

I have interviewed the applicant. There is definitely an opening in my Headquarters for this passed-over* Lieutenant, but please make sure that he does not slam the door on the way out.

Sub Lieutenant T tends to follow the path of least persistence.

The Catering Officer is very much like a puppy which wants to be loved, but only succeeds in upsetting dishes and ruining the furniture.

Lieutenant W is the sort of chap whose journey through life is characterised by pushing doors marked PULL.

This Assistant Secretary (Personnel) was fired, with some enthusiasm, because he wasn't fired with much enthusiasm at all.

---

* *Failed to be selected for promotion.*

This Instructor Officer is such a total drongo that his idea of an exciting night is to turn up the heat on his electric blanket.

This Officer Cadet works eight hours and sleeps eight hours a day; the only problem is that they are the same eight hours.

No one is Sub Lieutenant Z's equal at hitting the nail squarely on the thumb.

The Air Group Boss has strong views; he holds that *Vlad the Impaler* was something of a limp-wristed social worker.

It is amazing what this WRAF NCO can get away with, and still keep her amateur status.

The only thing that this Squadron Leader grows in his garden is – tired.

The Deputy Chief Instructor has stopped drinking coffee in the morning because it keeps him awake for the rest of the day.

Sub Lieutenant X is rusting on his laurels.

This Petty Officer Writer does most of his work sitting down, and that is where he shines.

Midshipman H never puts off until tomorrow what he can put off indefinitely.

For this Officer Cadet, the process of getting up in the morning is a major conflict between his mind and his mattress.

This potential recruit does not know how long he has been out of work, mainly because he cannot find his birth certificate.

Captain Y reminds me of my old Labrador; he will never learn any new tricks, nor will he move any faster.

My Correspondence Officer is almost dyslexic, but I am told that the dogged determination with which he tackles *Patience* and *Minesweeper* on the Ship's Office PC displays the kind of intellectual edge and computer skills desirable in today's Royal Navy.

This young trainee has become so lazy that even loafing appears to have become hard work.

Sub Lieutenant J's greatest pleasure in life is having lots to do, and then not doing it.

Wing Commander U will, if you are not careful, have the time of your wife at a party.

Unfortunately, when the wages of sin are paid, Captain C is likely to get time-and-a-half.

The only regular exercise that the Commander gets is when jumping to conclusions.

This young Cadet spends a lot of time shining up to the Head of Department, and very little effort on polishing off the work.

Not only does Officer Cadet M expect to get something for nothing, he also wants it gift-wrapped.

The Company Commander is an inspiration to us all. If he can make it, anyone can.

This civil servant claims to have an important job in our Archives department. As far as anyone else can see, he sits at his desk all day and collects cobwebs.

Space reserved for additional comments to be sent to Dr Rick Jolly at PO Box 42, Torpoint, Cornwall, PL11 2YR.

Please mark the envelope FAO Rick Jolly – IN CONFIDENCE!

88

Space reserved for additional comments to be sent to Dr Rick Jolly at PO Box 42, Torpoint, Cornwall, PL11 2YR.

Please mark the envelope FAO Rick Jolly – IN CONFIDENCE!

Space reserved for additional comments to be sent to Dr Rick Jolly at PO Box 42, Torpoint, Cornwall, PL11 2YR.

89

Please mark the envelope FAO Rick Jolly – IN CONFIDENCE!

Space reserved for additional comments to be sent to Dr Rick Jolly at PO Box 42, Torpoint, Cornwall, PL11 2YR.

Please mark the envelope FAO Rick Jolly – IN CONFIDENCE!

Space reserved for additional comments to be sent to Dr Rick Jolly at PO Box 42, Torpoint, Cornwall, PL11 2YR.

Please mark the envelope FAO Rick Jolly – IN CONFIDENCE!

Space reserved for additional comments to be sent to Dr Rick Jolly at PO Box 42, Torpoint, Cornwall, PL11 2YR.

Please mark the envelope FAO Rick Jolly – IN CONFIDENCE!

Space reserved for additional comments to be sent to Dr Rick Jolly at PO Box 42, Torpoint, Cornwall, PL11 2YR.

Please mark the envelope FAO Rick Jolly – IN CONFIDENCE!

Appendix i

THE FIRST CONFIDENTIAL REPORT

This letter was sent, from the field, to London in 1613, by Colonel L W Cass, commanding the 27th Regiment of Infantry. *'Annexed to the list of officers'*, he wrote, *'you will find all the observations I deem it necessary to make...'*

Lt Col Comm AD – *A good natured man.*

First Major CC – *A good man, but no officer.*

2nd Major JDW – *An excellent officer.*

Captains CH, ATC, BW, M – *All good officers.*

Captain S – *A man of whom all unite in speaking ill. A knave despised by all.*

Captain TE – *Indifferent – but promises well.*

Captain A R – *An officer of capacity, but impudent and a man of most violent passions.*

Captains DW, P – *Strangers, but little known in the regiment.*

First Lts JK, TD – *Merely good – nothing promising.*

First Lts WP, DS, JJR, RMcE – *Low vulgar men with the exception of P. From the meanest walks of Life possessing nothing of the character of officers or gentlemen.*

First Lt RPR – *Willing enough with small capacity.*

First Lt H – *Not yet joined regiment.*

Second Lt NGC – *A good officer but drinks hard and disgraces himself and the services.*

Second Lt SE – *An ignorant unoffending officer.*

Second Lt McC – *Raised from the ranks, ignorant, vulgar and incompetent.*

Second Lts P, JJB, TGS, OV – *Some from the ranks but all behave well and promise to make excellent officers.*

Second Lt JG – *A stranger in the regiment.*

Third Lts RG, M, C, McK – *All promoted from the ranks, low vulgar men, without any one qualification to recommend them, more fit to carry the hod than the epaulette.*

Third Lts JGS, FTW – *Promoted from the ranks, behave well, will make good officers.*

Ensign B – *The very dregs of the earth, unfit for anything under heaven. God only knows how the poor thing got an appointment.*

Ensigns JB, B – *Promoted from the ranks, men of no manners and no promise.*

Ensign CW – *From the ranks, a good young man who does well.*

Appendix ii

THE SOUTH ATLANTIC MEDAL ASSOCIATION

SAMA82 began its existence on April 2nd 1997, the fifteenth anniversary of the uninvited arrival of Argentine forces in the Falkland Islands. Soon afterwards, a task force was assembled in Great Britain and dispatched to the South Atlantic in order to restore Her Majesty's Sovereignty. On June 14 1982, Major General Jeremy Moore was able to announce to the world that the Falkland Islanders were once again living under the Government of their choice. Seventy four days of occupancy had elapsed.

Since those heady days 15 years ago many things have changed. The Islanders now have a measure of economic independence, and the geography of the capital, Stanley, has been radically reshaped. There is now a new airport complex, integrated with the garrison which continues to defend the Falklands against any aggressor. But most of the Task Force members also had their lives altered. Just under 780 were wounded, with injuries ranging from minor shrapnel scratches, through disfiguring burns, to amputation and loss of a limb or limbs.

Even those who were not wounded physically found that they had changed on their return home. A few were suffering from the cluster of severe symptoms known as Post Traumatic Stress Disorder; others merely had disturbed dreams. For nearly all veterans of the short but sharp South Atlantic conflict, November 11th's Remembrance Sunday now became an intense emotional experience, along with feelings of sadness and loss on specific anniversaries such as the land battles of Goose Green, Mount Harriet, Tumbledown, Two Sisters, Wireless Ridge and Mount Longdon – or the death in action of a friend and comrade elsewhere, perhaps at sea, or closer to shore at Fitzroy Cove, or in the Battle of San Carlos Water. Three Falkland Islanders also died in the fighting; two hundred and fifty two members of the Task Force did not return to their homes...

All these people are united in one thing. They, or their next-of-kin, received from Her Majesty's Government the South Atlantic Medal. It was awarded to all personnel who took part in operations in the South Atlantic for the liberation of South Georgia and the Falkland Islands. To qualify, the recipient had to have at least one full day's service in the Falkland Islands or South Georgia, or thirty days in the South Atlantic operational zone, including Ascension Island. Additionally, those who qualified under the first condition were awarded a rosette to wear on the medal ribbon.

What is perhaps surprising is that nearly 30,000 of these medals were awarded, underpinning the Government's seriousness in terms of generating the forces needed to carry out the difficult task of dislodging the Argentine invaders. The breakdown of medal awards was: Royal Navy 13,000; Royal Marines 3,700; Royal Fleet Auxiliary 2,000; Army 7,000; Royal Air Force 2,000 and Merchant Navy/Civilian 2,000.

The main purposes of SAMA82 are simply stated. We intend to maintain and promote a sense of pride and comradeship among all veterans of the South Atlantic campaign, and to keep them in touch with each other in a manner which respects both individual privacy and personal requirements. We also want to establish and maintain contact with other organisations involved in the welfare of the armed forces, and ensure that due consideration is given to the interests of South Atlantic veterans. SAMA82 will also investigate for consideration, by an appropriate organisation, any case of hardship or distress amongst South Atlantic veterans in which direct financial assistance is sought or recommended.

Finally, and perhaps most importantly for the majority of SAMA82's members, we desire most strongly to re-establish and strengthen links with the people of the Falkland Islands.

(a) **FULL MEMBERSHIP** will be reserved for those in possession of the South Atlantic Medal (1982). The subsidised fee, payable on joining, is £10.

(b) **SPECIAL MEMBERSHIP** will be granted on application (and without payment of fee) to the next of kin of those who died in the South Atlantic Campaign. These first 255 Membership numbers are allocated – and sacrosanct.

(c) **ISLAND MEMBERSHIP** has been secured for all Falkland Islanders.

(d) **HONORARY MEMBERSHIP** may be conferred by SAMA82's Executive on any individual who has been of great assistance in the management of SAMA's affairs. It may also from time to time be conferred on distinguished individuals who had a particular influence on the conduct or outcome of the South Atlantic campaign of 1982.

(e) **AFFILIATE MEMBERSHIP** may be granted to those with a special affection for the Islands and/or commitment to SAMA82's aims. The lifetime fee is £50, payable on joining.

All communication should be addressed to:

The Secretary,
South Atlantic Medal Association (1982)
PO Box 82, Blackwood, GWENT, NP2 0YE

Also published by Palamanando Press...

£8.95 plus
£1.05 p&p

For an order form which will allow you to have this book
personalised by the author, <u>either</u> write to:

Rick Jolly, c/o Palamanando Press,
PO Box 42, Torpoint, Cornwall PL11 2YR

and mark the envelope or postcard JACKSPEAK

<u>or else</u> send a fax message to 01503 230421
and we will fax an order form back to you.

(Regret credit cards not accepted – yet)